BALLOON IN A BOX

Coping with Grief

Written by
Thomas L. Rose

PEACE BE
WITH YOU ...
Tom

CCB Publishing
British Columbia, Canada

Balloon in A Box: Coping with Grief

Library and Archives Canada Cataloguing in Publication
Title: Balloon in a box : coping with grief / by Thomas L. Rose.
Names: Rose, Thomas L., 1940- author.
Issued in print and electronic formats.
ISBN 9781771435833 (softcover) – ISBN 9781771435017 (PDF)
Additional cataloguing data available from Library and Archives Canada

Cover artwork credit: Original cover design by Brock T. Rose.

Publisher: CCB Publishing
            British Columbia, Canada
            www.ccbpublishing.com

"To have become a deeper man is the privilege of those who have suffered."
- Oscar Wilde

Books by Thomas L. Rose

Balloon in A Box: Coping with Grief

The Secret is in the Pasta
A Murder Mystery Novel

Cooking Together Chinese Style

Cooking Together Quick and Easy

Cooking Together Revisited

Contents

"Now is your time of grief,
but I will see you again and you will rejoice,
and no one will take away your joy."
- John 16:22*

---

* All Scriptural quotes contained herein are from the 1987 version of the
KJV Bible and are in the Public Domain.

Introduction

"My Story"

The story begins August 11, 1962, when I married the most beautiful woman in the world, beautiful inside and out. She soon became not only my loving wife, but good companion and most of all my friend. We began a life journey of almost 58 years until her death in August of 2019, beginning my journey of grief. See page 111 for the obituary for Joyce E. Rose.

Over those 58 years we experienced the great joys of family, a son, daughter-in-law and granddaughter, and many friends. Our shared interest in cooking led us to author two cookbooks and to host a TV segment on the regional Fox morning show, *Cooking Together with Tom & Joyce*, for 13 years.

We also made appearances throughout the Midwest doing demonstrations and teaching cooking classes. After her death I completed the third cookbook *Cooking Together Revisited* with the assistance of my son, and it was dedicated to her memory with a portion of the proceeds going to Breast Cancer support projects. (Website: www.cookingtogether.com)

We made our last TV appearance after moving from our country home to a villa in the city in 2004. This was the year that Joyce was diagnosed with breast cancer, which was treated with chemotherapy and a mastectomy and again in 2005 with another mastectomy. With the support of family, friends, and her faith she was cancer free until 2017.

It occurred to me during the continuing process of my grief that many people, myself included before Joyce's death, do not understand grief or how to talk with someone experiencing grief. Especially grief because of the death of a spouse or a child. This would include some experts who have written books or published papers on the grief experience.

I did find some good books on the subject but most of these I found too clinical, like college professor clinical. I was looking for help in understanding my grief and how to handle it. A few of the better books were written by people who had experienced or were dealing with grief.

For several months I simply wrote down what I experienced every day. My feelings and reactions to the situation in my own simple words, not a clinical analysis. After reading these reactions a learned friend suggested I write this book. Maybe not the smartest thing I have ever done, but I accepted the challenge so here it is.

Please remember these are my experiences, analysis and opinions. I am not a doctor of Psychology, a trained grief counselor or professional of any kind. I am just a plain ordinary guy who has experienced the worst, the death of a loving spouse.

Tom

Update for Second Edition

After the publication of the first edition of this book my life has changed significantly. My original intention was to write the book, as my friend had suggested (almost insisted), print a couple hundred copies, give them to friends and maybe sell a few to cover the cost of printing. Well, it seems I have "caught lightning in a bottle" with my little book. I started receiving requests for media interviews including TV, radio, podcasts and print media. I also began to receive requests for personal speaking appearances. To date I have made over 75 appearances and have many more scheduled. I have spoken at churches, service clubs, retirement communities and even prisons. As a result, not only have I had personal conversations about grief with people after my speaking engagements, but I receive emails and personal calls from people asking for advice about their grief.

I received a call from a young man who said he had asked his mother, "How will I know I am in love?" and she gave him my book to read. I guess I have also written a love story. Probably true because without love there is no grief. It is sometimes said that love's everlasting gift is grief. As a result of all this my publisher suggested that I update the book into a second edition, including the things I have learned, my experiences and additional thoughts. So here it is, *Balloon in A Box: Coping with Grief*, second edition. Yes, my life has changed. At 82 years old I have become an author, speaker and grief adviser. Sharing all of this has now become my mission, my ministry and my quest.

What I have learned and experienced over the last year is that a griever must find a way to express themself, to find the words. Then they must share their feelings and say the words, and of course they need to know that the words have been heard.

"Every heart has its secret sorrows which the world knows not, and oftentimes we call a man cold, when he is only sad."
- Henry Wadsworth Longfellow

Grief is the response to loss, particularly to the loss of someone or some living thing that has died, to which a bond or affection was formed. Although conventionally focused on the emotional response to loss, grief also has physical, cognitive, behavioral, social, cultural, spiritual and philosophical dimensions.

Other names include: Mourning, Grieving, Bereavement

Grief (noun) is defined as:
- deep sorrow, especially that caused by someone's death.
- deep and poignant distress caused by someone's death.

* Source: https://en.wikipedia.org/wiki/Grief

Chapter One

"Grief"

Grief is a "heavy" word as are the other words associated with it like mourning, bereavement, etc. I wish there were less "depressing" words to describe your feelings when a spouse or child dies. I have searched the dictionary to find a new word for grief but failed. I might suggest the word "Pragma." Pragma is one of the seven types of love as described in the bible.

Pragma is often described as love built on commitment, understanding and long-term best interests. It is an everlasting love which is rooted in romantic feelings and companionship that continues to grow during one's lifetime, and it results in an intense feeling of deep affection for another person. The key words are: everlasting love, continues to grow, and feeling of deep affection.

I believe grief is Pragma, an everlasting love and a feeling of deep affection that continues to grow. It continues to grow even after your loved one has passed. It is as they say, "Absence makes the heart grow fonder." Even after these many months have passed since her death, if possible, I think I love her even more.

I believe I can show her and all those who knew her that my love for her continues to grow by what I do and what I have become, which are inspired by my memories of her. It shows by my love of family and how I treat all people, friends and strangers alike.

Yes, I continue to experience mourning and grief, but I remember how she would react to the same situation. Her friends know that one of her favorite sayings was: "It is what it is, so put on your 'big boy' pants and deal with it." She always told me this when things were not going the best for me. When she was diagnosed with breast cancer that is how she dealt with it, and even when she was told, "You have six to nine months to live," she dealt with it (she lived 2 ½ years). She was so strong. I am sure she was scared, but she went on in spite of the fear. She continued to live her life to the fullest and always placed the needs of others above her own needs. She was so strong.

We all experience grief in different ways. For some it is more difficult and they become depressed. This depression leads to other problems such as personality changes, irritability, frustration, confusion, etc. I am lucky I have never experienced depression because I have continued to draw on her strength.

We will continue to experience grief, but we must learn to turn it from a negative into a positive, Pragma! If not controlled, grief will take a lot of your energy. Don't allow that to happen. Don't waste your energy on grief, and instead use it for creating something positive. The cookbook, family cooking videos, the breast cancer support projects, and this book are taking my energy, so this is how I am handling grief.

Most people experience grief when someone they love dies, but if we are to heal, we must also mourn. The healing process is like a serious wound that heals but leaves a scar. Each time you look at the scar you remember the pain of the wound.

What is the difference between grief and mourning?

Grief is what we think and feel on the inside when someone we love dies. It is the internal meaning given to the experience of loss. Mourning is the outward expression of our grief. Grieving and mourning our loss are important because they allow us to 'free up' energy so that we might reinvest that energy elsewhere. Healthy grieving and mourning results in an ability to remember the importance of our loss with a newfound sense of peace, rather than pain.

The expression of grief and mourning for a deceased loved one is extremely personal. The amount of time spent in mourning will depend upon the individual's ability to process and cope with the loss. In upcoming chapters I will discuss this process in more detail.

You will probably experience sadness because of all the unfulfilled hopes, dreams and expectations you held with your spouse. I remembered our "bucket list" of places we wanted to go and things we wanted to do. This of course made me sad, but then I remembered all the places we did go and all the things we did together in our 59 years (one year dating, 58 years married) which makes me happy.

For a short time, I had trouble thinking, organizing and making decisions. While in the early stages of grieving and mourning, I suggest you do not make any major decisions (financial, moving, etc.). Wait 6 months to a year. You may have family and friends suggesting and pushing you to make these decisions... but resist!

You may feel anger. Angry with your loved one for leaving you, anger with God for taking them from you.

One day I woke up angry and I told both of them, God and Joyce, just how I felt... I let it all out! I actually injured my knee by kicking a chair. Did it make me feel better? Not really! Now I had to deal with the knee pain and my shame in talking to Joyce and God that way and I had to apologize, then I felt better! Probably one of my better healing moments, but the knee still hurt!

Lament is often defined as: a passionate expression of grief or sorrow. To Lament is to allow the suffering, grief, to come to the surface and express itself verbally. I guess that was what I was doing when I expressed my anger to God and Joyce. I then shared the experience with friends. To Lament is necessary to move forward. Get it out!

Your grief will depend on your relationship and how you perceive the loss. I lost a sister, but we were estranged and had not had any kind of relationship for over 25 years. I felt some grief as I made her final arrangements, but it passed quickly. However, I often have memories of her when we were kids. I have also lost both of my parents and, of course, I miss them very much. I guess I felt my first real grief after their deaths. My father lived to almost ninety and my mother ninety-eight. They lived very full lives.

As I said, my parents' deaths were the first real grief I had ever dealt with, but the death of my wife resulted in 10 to 100 times more than the most grief I had ever experienced. The pain, the sadness and the loneliness were unlike anything I had ever felt in my life. But "it is what it is," and I am dealing with it with the support of my family, friends, and God's love.

I am certain I will never completely recover from her loss, but I do understand that I must adjust and move forward. In the beginning I tried to block out my thoughts of her, but now I understand that it is okay to think of her daily. It is said that "the best defense is a good offense." Every morning when I wake, I spend a few minutes thinking of how I will handle grief today. That any grief experienced will be Pragma. I will control the grief with my many projects and daily chores... it will not control me! I then get out of bed and say aloud, "Hey, Joyce, it is going to be a good day." Some days are good and others not so good. But with each passing week/month I am having more good days than bad.

Some widows and widowers experience after-death communication with the loved one. It is a subject that grief experts have now begun to explore. I'm not sure how I feel about this, but in my dreams we do talk. Maybe it is communication or maybe it's just a dream. When I misplace my cell phone, I use the landline to locate it. The caller identification on the cell phone displays "Joyce" as the caller. I want to hit the redial button and see if she will answer!

In the summer of 2020, I was diagnosed with COVID and for fourteen weeks spent most of my time in bed either sleeping or looking out the window. During this time, I was able to analyze my grief and learn to somewhat control it. I could, most of the time, control my dreams by thinking of good memories before I fell asleep, thereby creating pleasant dreams. However, sometimes the nightmare of spending three weeks in Hospice watching her die and then holding her hand as she took her final breath rears its ugly head.

Those three weeks in Hospice at the hospital (she did not want to come home after she had made the decision) were the most difficult weeks in my life. I stayed with her 24/7 with some relief from my family when I could come home, shower, change clothes and eat.

Sitting with her day-by-day, the first 2 weeks we would talk about the family and things she wanted me to do. During the last few days I would hold her hand when she slept. It was not a peaceful sleep because I could feel her pain as I held her hand. I had always prayed for her recovery, but now I was asking God to please take her from the pain. I even whispered to her that it was okay that she could go with God and rest in peace.

As I sat with her in hospice, I kept wondering why God was allowing her to suffer. Why not just take her from the pain? Now I think I understand it was so I would learn to become more like her. Use her strength to make me a better person. She was suffering for me! God had done this with his Son to make us all better people.

I believe my grief had begun long before she died. Sitting in that room watching her die, I experienced many of the grief symptoms: heartache, loneliness, sadness, and many others.

I quickly realized after her death the grief was not only emotional but affected me mentally, spiritually and also physically. At first, I was very anxious, nervous, with an inability to relax. I had sweaty hands and feet. I was beginning to sleep for extended periods of time. I was going to bed at 9:00 pm and not getting out of bed until 9:00 am. Then I took a 1-to-2-hour nap in the afternoon. Much different from my normal pattern of 10:30 pm until 6:30 am with no nap.

Some people have told me they experienced the opposite, sleeping too little. I have managed to adjust my sleep pattern to 10:00 pm to 8:00 am, which is still an extended time and maybe also a short nap, probably because I am getting older.

The loss of a spouse is sometimes unexpected. Even when it is expected it still strikes fear and pain in our hearts. Joyce's death was expected. But I experienced the sudden fear: what was I going to do without her, without her strength? And the pain was almost unbearable. I'd never be able to forget that moment or be able to get rid of the heartbreak. I loved her very much and she was gone. I would never see her again, talk with her or hold her hand, share cooking, family... she would never be with me again. The fear I felt made me very unsure of my future. I was lost!

If this pain is to be my life, if this is living, then I don't want to live anymore. But deep down I was wrong. At that point I knew I needed to process all that was happening to me in a healthy way. I needed to sort through all the fear, questions, emotions and thoughts that were sapping my energy.

I did not want to stay stuck in this place. I must believe in myself by resisting the fear and having faith in my ability to cope with the grief. I wanted to feel normal again, but I knew that normal would never be again.

The tears would come, I would have good and bad days, and nothing would be normal. At this point I began my journey through grief. In the beginning it was a journey through hell. But as I gained control of my life things became clear about how I was to proceed.

"Hear my cry O God;
Attend my prayer.
From the end of the earth
I will cry to you.
When my heart is overwhelmed;
Lead me to the rock that is higher than I."
-Psalm 61:1-2

I kept saying, "Do not be afraid, do not think: what next? Instead, gather your strength and move through every new grief event with courage. Draw on her strength and let it guide you forward with your life."

Bottom line, grief is a very complex subject. Experts, after years of serious studies, cannot tell us when it will end or if it will ever end. My opinion is that it will always be with us in some form. Maybe Pragma, an everlasting love, and a feeling of deep affection that continues to grow.

"Grief is like living two lives.
One is where you pretend that everything is alright, and
the other is where your heart silently screams out in pain."
- Author Unknown

Unless you have been there you do not truly understand.

Chapter Two

"It Will Get Better"

To say that people are uncomfortable with mourning is an understatement! Remember mourning is the outward expression of our grief. Think about the times when you were grieving and tried to share how you were feeling with others. Sometimes your friend or family member would simply listen, without analysis, criticism or judgment. More likely the person would try to give you logical reasons not to feel bad, tell you about someone else who they thought had an even worse situation or told you that "it will get better," or even, "you'll get over it in time!"

Those who listened allowed you to express and even release some of that emotional pain making you feel better. The others, who tried to talk you out of that pain experience left you feeling that no one really understood or even cared to understand your pain and heartache. **Unless you have been there you do not truly understand.**

"Don't let anyone who hasn't been in your shoes
tell you how to tie them."
- Author Unknown

"It will get better." So far in my experience and that of others to whom I have talked, this is not true, it doesn't get better, just different! Yes, it changes as you learn to live with it by controlling it and making the memories happy ones. Then you will find yourself experiencing Pragma.

When I posted on Facebook about grief, I received this response from my son: *"I have heard it said that love's everlasting gift is grief. Dad, your love for her will continue forever."*

"You'll get over it in time." This is probably the worst thing you can say. Maybe I don't want to get over it, maybe I just want to experience it and grow because of it. I spent 59 years of my life with this person. How do I move on with my life without taking these 59 years with me?

I had a friend who lost her husband. She was having a tough time because they were not only husband and wife but business partners. She became overwhelmed with the grief and the business decisions. I told her to take a deep breath and tell herself, "I'm okay!" Now when she sees that I am having issues I get an email that just says, "I'm okay," and it really helps.

What do you say to the spouse when you go to a funeral? It's always tough for me. Do you say I'm so sorry, or he or she was great, or maybe how are you doing? Now that I have experienced the situation, I think the best thing to say is, "I love you and I'm here if you need me."

I went to a friend's funeral the other day and that is what I told his wife as I gave her a hug. I also told her that she should remember all the "hugs" she was getting that day because she was going to need them in the days to come.

It is hard to explain the loneliness and heartache to someone if they have not been there. It is probably easier to explain the "Holy Trinity" or E=mc2. The dictionary defines heartache as: *emotional anguish or grief, typically caused by the loss or absence of someone loved.* The dictionary defines anguish as: *severe mental or physical pain or suffering.*

We have all experienced heartache at one time or another, but have you ever really tried to explain it? To me it was/is more like someone kicking me in the solar plexus. It takes my breath away and the pain brings tears to my eyes. So, if someone wants to know how you really feel ask them if they would like to have you kick them in the solar plexus!

The actions and comments of our friends and family are all meant to bring us peace and resolution. So, we must remember if they have not been there then they don't understand, but we know they love us and don't like seeing us in pain.

Things not to say to someone who is mourning:

- It will get better.
- It will pass with time.
- At least he/she is no longer in pain.
- Everything happens for a reason.
- I understand how you feel. (No, you don't.)
- Well, you had her for 59 years.
- God needed her up there more than down here.

Please, please do not ask, "How are you doing?" I believe that is the worst thing you can say!! At least in my case I felt that way. Of course, when someone at the visitation asked this question all I could say was, "Okay, I'm doing okay," when I really wanted to say, "How do you think I'm doing? My wife died, I'm scared, confused, sad, angry and alone. My heart aches and my stomach hurts. Other than that, I'm just fine." I understand they meant well, but please just don't do it. Don't ask, "How are you doing?"

Don't try and fix it. You're there for support. It is not your job to "fix it." Don't try and give solutions. Don't use the terms "passed away" or "loved one." Instead, use the person's name, Joyce, and she died, she did not just pass away! Don't use the term "lost" which could mean if you search hard, you might find him/her.

Someone said to me, "You are still young. You will find someone to share your life with." I was 78, and I was not ready to find someone new! I'm still not ready, and I'm not sure I will ever be ready.

One of the worst things I heard was when a friend who lost a young child was told, "Well, at least you have two other children." Unbelievable!

Things to consider saying to someone who is mourning:

- Nothing I could say would make this any easier.
- I am here for you.
- I am praying for you and your family.
- I am sorry for your loss.
- Say nothing and just give a hug.
- I love you, I am here for you.
- Or best, say, "I love you," and then give a hug.

Saying "I love you" and giving a hug says it all. Trust me, I know what it meant and still means to me. We had over 450 people at the viewing. It was not really a viewing because she wanted a closet casket. Everyone tried to express their sympathy to the family, but I simply remember the hugs and when they said, "I love you." I use the memory of those hugs to help me face the grief. Knowing that there are people who care about me means a lot. I truly love them.

So it is not going to get better, just different. It will be different because you will be different. You will never be the same as you were before the death of your spouse.

"Time heals old pain, while it creates new ones."
- Proverb

The changes may be subtle. You may not recognize them at first but your friends and family will. I noticed that I was not as interested or passionate about some things as I had before her death. I still enjoy playing golf but not with the passion I did previously. I still enjoy watching sports on TV but not with the same intense interest I did previously. In fact, I will now go for days without turning on the TV.

I have had a keen interest in cooking for many years, but in this case it intensified. Maybe I have become more passionate about cooking because it was something we shared, and I want to hang on to that. It may be that it is because food and cooking are something we share together as a family, and I want to stay close to family.

A couple of my friends said I seem to listen more and concentrate more on what is being said. They said that my contributions to the conversation appear to be coming from a deeper thought process. Wow, I guess in the past I just talked but said nothing worthwhile? May be true!

I do know that I have become more cerebral. I have spent a

lot of time thinking. Sometimes I sit for extended periods of time just thinking. I think about Joyce and our time together, the family and what their future may hold for them, my friends and of course God.

I always liked to read, but not with the passion for reading I have developed over the past few months. I have always read mystery, spy novels and of course cookbooks and cooking magazines, but now I enjoy self-help and nonfiction as well. Books like *I Heard God Laugh*, which I will reference later in this book, to *The Autobiography of Santa Claus*. I even go to the library every couple of weeks. In the past it was probably once a year. And I search for things on the Internet that I wish to understand.

One of the biggest changes was to take on the challenge of writing this book. Never in the past would I have considered taking the time from golf and TV sports to do something like this. No way! The best things to take away from this chapter are: *"It's not going to get better it's just going to change,"* and, *"Love's everlasting gift is grief."*

"Love never fails. But where there are prophecies, they will cease; where there are tongues, they will be stilled; where there is knowledge, it will pass away. And now these three remain: faith, hope and love. The greatest of these is love."
- 1 Corinthians 13:8-13

Update for Second Edition

After writing, publishing, and speaking about this book on grief, I had thought grief would never truly end. At this point I have met several hundred people helping me to understand it doesn't get better, only different. Over time it may become gentler but sometimes it inflicts a sharp pain. I know that grief will last as long as love does because Pragma is a continuing love. I continue to experience the ebb and flow of grief with its sorrow, joy, pain and memories of love.

Unfortunately, I have attended several funerals and visitations recently, and I was able to observe the discomfort and anxiety of people attending. They did not know what to say to the family of the loved one. I overheard the favorite of, "How are you doing?" many, many times and also, "They are in a better place."

As grief changes, so do we.

Chapter Three

"Balloon in A Box"

There are an unlimited number of books and resources written by "experts" all with different approaches to the subjects of grief and mourning. Many are written by people who have never experienced the loss of a spouse. They have no clue as to what it really feels like but tell us how we feel and how to handle the situation. Most tell us that it will get better and end sometime in the future. As you know by now, I do not agree.

I guess the question is: "How does it become different?" For me it was like a "balloon in a box." In the beginning the balloon touched all six sides of the box, scrambling all the emotions and feelings. As time passed the balloon became smaller, floating around in the box and sometimes it touched a side bringing back memories, some good and some bad. When it touched a corner (3 sides), it brought out that confusing entanglement of emotions.

Following are some examples: Maybe when it touches a side, a memory of your first date with your spouse flashes back to you, or if it touches a corner, you suddenly feel sad and lonely. The trick is to keep the balloon from touching the corners and just the sides with pleasant memories.

In the beginning the balloon is touching all 6 sides of the box. It is painful and demands action. Why would you want to stay there? At some point you will grow tired of the pain and decide to take charge of yourself. When you are strong enough there will be motivation to gain control of your emotions and establish stability.

Grab that string attached to the balloon and guide it to where you want it to go and bring back those pleasant memories. Keep it from touching the corners. Sometimes it will, but try your best.

Before Joyce died, I thought grief was an experience that would decrease and finally go away. I thought all an individual needed to do was talk with a pastor, councilor or friend and they would be cured. I thought it was like having the flu. Visit the doctor, take the prescribed medicine and get well. Guess what, I was wrong.

It requires concentrated effort and thought. Time does not heal, and emotions do not stabilize without a great deal of work. There is no shortcut through grief. Working through grief is a gradual process and has no time schedule. It is hard work, but you will feel better each day. Hold the grief inside and it stays with you. Face it head-on, work through it, and although it never really ends you will feel it less because you control it. You must face up to grief because it requires a response. If you try to hide from it, you will find no relief. But face it on your own terms, maybe using the "balloon in a box."

Life changes quickly. Even if you are aware that a change is coming, it is still a shock. I was stunned by the changes in my life. I thought I had prepared myself for life without her, but again I was wrong, and the loss was almost unbearable. After 59 years together I was now alone. Even though it was August, the house seemed cold. The nights were long and days even longer. I realized that I needed to resume somewhat of a "normal" life with my friends and family. I needed them to understand my grief. After six weeks away from it, I began playing golf again. But it was not the same. Nothing was the same!

I had a long talk with myself, Joyce and God trying to figure out how I really felt and what I should do. I was avoiding the grief, trying to hide from it. What I really needed to do was face it and share it with my family and friends. I began to understand that it would take time, and a certain amount of the grief would remain with me forever. I have spoken with many people who have experienced the death of a spouse and they all tell me that they have those moments when it returns. One lady said, "It's been 25 years and I think of him every day. I still miss him very much." Another said, "It has been 18 years and I have remarried, but I think of him often and his sense of humor and practical jokes. There was a little of the devil in him. I cry a little."

I said, "Okay grief, bring it on. I am ready!" I will cry, feel lonely, get angry, etc., and mourn my loss. I will learn to share my feelings and accept the changes in my life. I will allow my love for her to continue to grow, and I'll use that love to move me forward. As the grief changed, I found myself changing, and I believed I was a better person than I was before she died.

In the beginning grief is overwhelming and exhausting and as it progresses you become lost and disoriented, like being lost in the woods at night. You experience confusion, anxiety, fear, intense pain and loneliness. You feel like no one really understands, and you are probably right. You experience a disconnection with family and friends. What you need is to talk, be heard, and to know that someone really cares. They do not need to understand, but just care.

Let the tears flow, washing away the pain of grief, and then you will begin to experience a new focus on life forming new routines, relationships and interests. You may develop a greater understanding of love, a desire to help others and a stronger faith in God.

Grief is unpredictable, hard to understand and difficult to handle. As you journey down the path to healing, you must take it one step at a time. Grief will test you in ways you have never experienced. Be patient.

How do you control the "balloon in the box?"

First you need to establish contact with the "string." You need to organize your thoughts, set your plans (very short-term, day-by-day), taking each day as it comes with its weapon of grief.

Once you can do this you will have the "string" in your grasp. Sometimes it will slip away and confusion and fear will return. You will need to reorganize your thoughts. Regrip the string, maybe tie it to your finger so it can't slip away. Now you will be able to slowly control your grief and make progress with your life without your spouse or loved one. Use your memories to build your new life.

Like golf, tennis or any other sport, the more you play the better you become at it. The more you use the string, the better you will become at controlling it. It is a very slow process. I have been working on it for over two years, but sometimes that "balloon" just seems to go where it wants. So, I still experience those unpleasant emotions of grief, but each time it happens I learn a little bit more about how to control it.

Grief is never going away, and we will always feel the heartache, the pain and loneliness. You will still cry, however now the tears will bring you relief.

"We need never be ashamed of our tears."
- Charles Dickens

So, the better we learn to control the "balloon" the easier it will be for us to move forward. Events will happen that cause you to lose control of the "balloon."

A smell, a picture, the most unexpected thing can trigger a memory, but with the control you have developed you will be able turn these from unpleasant to pleasant memories.

Hold on to that string and move forward, slowly!

Once when I was explaining my "balloon in a box" analogy someone questioned, "Wouldn't it be better just to pull on the string and remove the balloon from the box and just release it?" By letting the balloon drift off into space, wouldn't that end your grief?

My answer was yes you could do that, and you would put an end to your grief. But remember, grief is love and love is grief. Without grief we would not have love, and that balloon is your total package of love. It contains all your memories, your first and last kiss (all the ones in between), your first and last argument (and all the ones in between). If you release that balloon, you lose all your memories. Without the memories you would have no grief.

Do you really want to sacrifice all your memories to end your grief? **Not me, I want the memories, and for that I will endure the grief.**

"There is no greater sorrow than to recall happiness in times of misery."
- Dante Alighieri

Update for Second Edition

In the first edition of my book, I had described the balloon in the box getting smaller as time passed, but I now realize the balloon did not get smaller. In fact, it may have actually slightly increased in size as more memories were added. What actually occurs is that as you move forward the box becomes larger. Learning to control the balloon in a larger box makes it easier to handle the grief. But as I have said many times throughout the book grief never ends, it becomes different, and you learn to control it, but it will always be there. So, keep the string tied to your finger so you can control the grief as you move forward with your loved one, not without them because all your memories are there in the balloon.

"I don't want to be at the mercy of my emotions...
I want to dominate them."
- Oscar Wilde

Chapter Four

"Feelings and Emotions"

My question was what comes first Feelings or Emotions? So, I did some research. The answer is emotions come first then feelings. Feelings are triggered by emotions and shaped by our own experiences, beliefs, memories and thoughts. The feeling is a side product of your brain experiencing the emotion and giving it a certain meaning. Then moods develop from a combination of feelings.

The fundamental difference between feelings and emotions is that feelings are experienced consciously, while emotions show themselves consciously or subconsciously. While emotions are bodily reactions generated by the brain, feelings are the conscious experience of these emotional reactions. Wow, I guess I understand, but bottom line here is that those emotions, feelings and moods can be very intense when it comes to grieving.

One of my favorite new authors (new to me) is Matthew Kelly. In his book *Life Is Messy** he explains that "feelings are visitors to the heart" and suggests we welcome them. Further, he explains that "each feeling comes to teach you something very specific. They are only passing through. Unless you ignore them. This detains them unnecessarily. You cannot get them to leave by ignoring them, avoiding them or pretending

---

* *Life is Messy* by Matthew Kelly © 2021, Blue Sparrow, used with permission.

they don't exist. They will stay until you attend to them."

In my experience with grief, I tend to agree with Matthew Kelly. Each time an emotion/feeling has inserted itself into my life I have had to deal with it or else it lingers in my brain. This has sometimes created "moods" that created problems for me to think clearly and function.

So how many emotions are there? According to American psychologist Dr. Robert Plutchik, he believes that we have 34,000 emotions that we can experience. However, normally most people experience the eight basic emotions of joy, sadness, acceptance, disgust, fear, anger, surprise and anticipation. Understanding how to deal with these basic emotions is important because otherwise most people will revert to what is known as the fight or flight response.

I am sure there are some people who spend years not understanding the depths of their emotions and feelings. I was one of those people who did not understand until Joyce died and I began to experience grief. As we discussed in earlier chapters grief is love. Until her death I did not understand the depth of my love for her.

When I first realized I loved her and that she loved me, I thought I understood at that time how deeply I felt I loved her, but I did not. When we were married, I was sure my love could not be any deeper, but again I did not understand. When we were expecting our son and he was born, I was sure this was the ultimate love, but again I was wrong. When our son was married and we were blessed with a granddaughter, I knew we had reached a love that could go no deeper, but I again did not understand. It has been 2 ½ years since Joyce died, and I now understand that with the intense emotions and feelings brought on by grief there is no end to the depth of love.

I would be remiss if I did not, in a chapter on Emotions and Feelings, include a discussion of Love. My question was: "Is love an emotion or a feeling?" We have established that Grief is Love and Love is Grief, that without either the other does not exist.

But what is love? Is it an emotion or feeling? In the dictionary Love is described as: "An intense feeling of deep affection. Feeling deep affection for (someone)."

Affection is described as: "A feeling of liking and caring for someone or something; tender attachment; fondness."

In my research I found that some experts suggest that love is a basic human emotion just like happiness or anger, while others believe that it is a feeling triggered by an emotion. We established that feelings are triggered by emotions. What is the emotion that triggers the feeling of love?

Further research suggested that the emotion of euphoria, and the release of a jumble of chemicals in the brain, including dopamine (pleasure), adrenaline (fight or flight) and norepinephrine (alertness), can make being in love a very deep crazy feeling. So now I needed to get a description of euphoria: "A feeling or state of intense excitement and happiness."

So, we did all that research and we are back to Grief is Love and Love is Grief, that without either the other does not exist. And, Pragma, the intense love that continues to grow.

Many years ago at a funeral for a classmate and friend a priest in his homily, direct to the deceased's wife, said:

"You will grieve, for grief is the final act of love. Those who grieve deeply have loved deeply. Through grief's darkness you will see the light of love. It will take great

courage to face the grief but your continuing love will give you the strength to handle your journey, making you a better person because you have experienced love."

As I began to understand my feelings, emotions and the depth of love, I understood how difficult it would be to live my life without her to the fullest. I needed to fully understand to be the "new" me. I needed to conquer grief in order to be free.

Yes, I needed to control the grief. That's what I must do now, "I gotta be me," and live my life "my way."

So how do I do it? With God's grace and Joyce's strength I believe it is going to happen. I have set my priorities and I am focused on them. I am moving forward with her, not without her. As I mentioned earlier, I am a new person, a better person because of her.

In Chapter Two I outlined some of the changes I have experienced. I have embraced and expanded these changes. I have developed many new interests, made new friends, and learned to love and enjoy everyone and everything. You must move forward...

My family has been fantastic through my journey of grief. Even though they also grieve they have given me three things: love, freedom and understanding. They have never told me what to do or questioned anything I have said or done. They have not tried to "fix it' or smothered me with attention. They have always been there when I have needed their support, but they have allowed me to be "me" and live my life "my way."

Psychological research reveals that emotions have potent, pervasive, predictable, sometimes harmful effects on decision making. Emotions and feelings have influenced some of my judgments and choices over the past two-plus years.

Fortunately, none of these have had a negative influence on my life. My suggestion, as I said earlier, is not to make "snap" decisions. Take time and think any major decisions through before acting on them.

When grieving, going with your "gut feeling" when faced with a big decision, is probably not the best way to go. Step back and make a careful list of the pros and cons, then you can make a more reasoned decision. Intuition can be great but even when you think your decisions are based on logic and common sense, they are often steered by emotion.

It's important to recognize how our thoughts and emotions control our bodies and behavior. Understanding how emotions played into my decision-making process helped me. Hopefully, I find the perfect balance between reason and intuition, helping me to make life choices that better serve my needs.

Different emotions affect decisions in different ways. When I was feeling sad, I was willing to settle for things that weren't necessarily best for me physically, mentally or financially. Emotional decision making can affect not just the outcome of a decision, but the speed at which you make it. Do not confuse quick decisions with strength. You must be decisive but only after considering all the facts and understanding how it will and could affect your future.

My doctor friend said when you are feeling stressed, anxious, or upset, you may not take care of your health as well as you should. Poor emotional health can weaken your body's immune system. This makes you more likely to get colds and other infections during emotionally difficult times. So, I tried to take care of myself physically as well as mentally.

He also pointed out that emotional resilience is one's ability to adapt to stressful situations or crises, like grief. More resilient people are able to "roll with the punches" and adapt to adversity without lasting difficulties; less resilient people have a harder time with stress and life changes.

You must build emotional resilience and bounce back from the negative feelings and emotions. The challenge lies in the ability to get back up after we fall and move on with our lives.

Update for Second Edition

One of the unique experiences I had in the last 12 months was speaking to participants in a jail drug rehabilitation program. In the program the inmates were required to participate in an extensive education program. The director of the program had set it up that I would speak then would give each of the 14 gentlemen in the program my book. Their assignment was to read the book and prepare questions or comments for my return visit in two weeks.

After my presentation each one of the guys came up to me, I thought to shake my hand, but to my surprise they all gave me a hug. It was a very emotional experience, so much so that when I returned to my car, I was overcome with emotion and began crying.

When I returned, I was impressed with how intelligent and intellectual their questions and comments were. In fact, so much so that I commented, "These are so intelligent and intellectual, what the hell are you guys doing here?" They all commented, "Well, Mr. Rose, we screwed up."

As each asked a question or made a comment, a discussion followed. I noticed one young man, John, had not commented so I asked if he had a question. He said, "I feel bad because my father died, and I am not grieving for him." I asked, "John, did you love your father?" He answered, "No, I hated him. He was a drunken bum, he beat us, my mother, sisters and me. No, I did not love him." I reminded him that "grief is love and without love there can be no grief." I told him it was not his fault that he did not grieve, but it was his father's fault because there was no love between them. He then shared his grief over the loss of his mother.

After speaking at LITE, Living in Transition Effectively, the group then used my book as a 6-week workshop. The moderator used statements from the book as prompts for writing a journal. After each prompt the participants were offered the opportunity, not required, to share their writing. I attended one of their sessions and was amazed at the emotional resilience of the members as they shared their stories. The group consisted of people who had lost spouses and children, as well as those who were recovering drug addicts and who were in transition from jail back into society, even those moving forward after a divorce.

Yes, from speaking about my book and my grief journey, I have experienced the emotions and feelings of many wonderful people. I cherish all of those experiences and hope that I have helped make their journeys a little less difficult.

"You cannot prevent the birds of sorrow from flying over your head, but you can prevent them from building nests in your hair."
- Old Chinese Proverb

Chapter Five

"Coping with Grief"

As I said in the last chapter, "Okay grief, bring it on I am ready!"

I was ready to cope with my grief, but how? I did my research at the library and online to put together my plan of attack. If you are facing grief, here is what I learned. Remember, grief is different for everyone, but you'll want to try some or all of these:

Patience:

I have been patient, allowing my grief to proceed at its own pace. I am trying not to get frustrated or judge myself for not healing as quickly as I or others think I should.

Feel:

I learned to allow myself to "feel." Feel all the emotions. The pain of your grief won't go away faster if you ignore it. Trying to do that could only make things worse. You need to actively face the pain. As is often said, grieving is the only solution to dealing with your grief.

Experience:

I am allowing myself, as much as it sometimes hurts, to experience the pain. Although I am sure many of my friends are thinking I should "get over it," I am allowing myself to fully experience the feelings.

Share:

I am continuing to talk about my sadness with friends and family. I have found it helps me release my feelings. I hope they understand and will be patient with me.

> *"Although it's difficult today to see beyond the sorrow, may looking back in memory help comfort you tomorrow."*
> - Author unknown

Support:

I joined a support group at my church, and it has been very helpful sharing my experiences with others who are also grieving. I guess *"there is strength in numbers."*

Forgive:

I try to avoid blaming myself for the things I didn't do or say when she was alive, and instead concentrate on the good memories.

Outlets:

Someone suggested I express my feelings through a creative

outlet. Since I have no art or music talent, they suggested I write a journal of my thoughts and feelings. And then, it turned into this book. Try writing it down, it really helps.

Physical Activity:

I find that physical activities help me cope with my feelings. I walk and I play golf. Smacking that golf ball around helps release some of the frustration and anger.

Social Activity:

Socializing with friends and family has been a great help to cope with my grief. Since I enjoy it, cooking for friends has been valuable for me in the grieving process.

Daily Routine:

Keeping my routine of daily activities has helped me structure my time and keep me connected to the "now," the present.

Love:

Even after her death, my love for her continues to grow and I embrace it. That feeling of continuing love helps dull the pain of loss and grief. This is Pragma, which is an everlasting love rooted in romantic feelings and companionship that continues to grow. "Try it you will like it!"

> "For though we have never yet seen God,
> when we love each other, God lives in us
> and his love within us grows ever stronger."
> - 1 John 4:12

Connect:

I continue to connect with her, thinking about the advice and strength she gave me. When I am cooking, I am reminded of the things she taught me. The simple little things that brought flavor to the food along with her knowledge of herbs and spices.

Health:

One of the most important things I have learned so far is to maintain both my physical and mental health. Grieving has been emotionally and physically exhausting. Getting enough sleep, eating properly and exercising have been of significant value in my battle with grief.

Prayer:

I pray every day for the strength and understanding to confront my grief. "God give me her strength." You may want to write your own prayer to express your unique feelings.

Stages of Grief:

I read about the different stages of grief: denial, anger, bargaining, depression, and acceptance. However, I found that grief isn't nearly that predictable. To me it felt like an emotional roller coaster. Don't think that you should be feeling a certain way at a certain time. Grief doesn't always move through stages.

Be Prepared:

I wasn't prepared. Some days the pain of grief was more manageable than others. Then a reminder such as a recipe, a photo, a piece of music, or a simple memory would trigger a wave of painful emotions again. Be prepared, hold the string of that balloon and move it where you want it to go.

Moving On:

I found it difficult to continue forward with my life. I learned that it doesn't mean my pain would end or Joyce would be forgotten. She had become a part of me. Maybe the pain will become easier to bear, but the memories and the love for her will always remain. Moving on doesn't mean forgetting!

Friends and Family:

I had always leaned on Joyce for support, she was my strength. Now I have learned to lean on friends and family. In the grief process I have built some new friendships. I now feel comfortable telling others what I need. I focus on those who are "good listeners."

The most important thing is to feel heard by those you confide in. But the raw emotion of your grief can make some people very uncomfortable. I always turn to those who are better able to listen and provide comfort.

> *"Blessed are those who mourn,*
> *for they shall be comforted."*
> *- Matthew 5:4*

Legacy:

Hopefully I am building a legacy with the "Cooking Together for a Cure" campaign and fundraiser whereby the family is providing head-wear packages to breast cancer patients having chemo treatments. We also provide grants to patients with financial problems.

If you don't want to start your own campaign, then volunteer for a cause that was important to your loved one or donate to a charity they supported. It has helped me add a sense of purpose as I move forward with my life. I promise it will help you.

Remember:

I am remembering Joyce by continuing to do the things we did together like cooking, walks, shopping and visiting our favorite places. And of course, that glass of wine in the evening while we "cooked together." These things have helped soften the pain and are helping me heal.

When Joyce died, I didn't lose her all at once. I lost her in pieces... her scent faded from the pillows and even from the closet and drawers.

Gradually all the parts of her were gone. And when the day came, I was overwhelmed with the feeling that she was gone forever, but not from my memory.

There should be a rule book that says it is alright to wake up crying, but only for a month. That after 60 days you will no longer turn around, certain you have heard her call out your name.

That it's alright if you feel the need to clean out her closet and clean out her desk. That it's okay to measure the time she has been gone, the way we once measured our anniversaries and birthdays.

"And the God of all grace, who called you to his eternal glory in Christ, after you have suffered a little while, will himself restore you and make you strong, firm and steadfast."
- Peter 5:10

Update for Second Edition

Coping with Grief as we discussed is very difficult, but with the help of my family and friends the road now seems less bumpy. My speaking engagements with my book and all the wonderful people I have met and who have shared their stories, including those who have told me I have helped them cope, have helped me cope with my grief.

I just went to see the movie *A Man Called Otto* with Tom Hanks... great movie! Everyone who is coping with grief needs to see this movie. It helped me understand that I need to continue moving forward with her love and leave the pain behind. Thanks Otto.

Sharing is healing.

Chapter Six

"Sharing Helps"

Sharing your own grief experience and memories with others can help you in understanding the uniqueness and similarities of your own grief journey with theirs. Sharing your story can help both you and others heal.

The need is there, and I found myself wanting to talk about the grief and my memories. It sometimes causes tears and I believe that is a good thing. It has been said: "Tears are nature's way of healing our emotional wounds."

"Grief shared is halved,
Joy shared is doubled."
- An Old Proverb

Sharing my memories of Joyce with friends and family has helped me to feel a sense of peace. Just talking about grief is very important to avoid suppressing your emotions. I have also witnessed that my sharing has prompted friends to share stories of their deceased loved ones. It occurred to me that maybe they were experiencing grief that had been "bottled up" inside them for an extended period of time. These conversations have brought tears, laughter, joy, and again a sense of peace.

Seek out people who have gone through their own grief process and absorb what they have to teach. Learn how to handle your grief from their experience. Understand that each person's grief is different and apply that experience where it fits into your grief journey.

Along my grief journey I have heard and shared memories and grief experiences. I would like to share some of those experiences with you. They may help you to understand grief a little better.

I will call her "B." She said her husband was ill for a length of time before his death, and he told her before he died that he needed to "help her develop a backbone." He had always been the strong one and handled all the family business and problems. As she said, "If I got a bad meal in a restaurant or poor service from a business, I would just let it pass." As he would tell me, "Don't let people take advantage. So, before his death he helped me develop a backbone. Now I am a tough old broad."

Here is what a gentleman named "R" had to say: "It's been 15 years and not a day goes by that I don't think of her. Damn I miss her."

Let's call this next person lady "C." She lost a 6-year-old son in a fire. She said, "There I was standing in the yard holding one of my three sons, the other was at a sleep over, watching my house burn to the ground with my 6-year-old son inside. And then I had to call my husband who was on the road and tell him what happened. How can I ever forget?" Even with my grief experience with Joyce's death, there is no way I can understand her grieve of losing a child in a fire. I believe he would be 30+ years old now, so their grief continues even after 25 years.

Similar to "C" is the story of a college friend who was playing with his sons, ages 4, 6, and 8 in a canoe in about 5 feet of water at the end of the pier at their lake cottage. The canoe flipped over. He knew the boys 6 and 8 were good swimmers so he went under and pulled the 4-year-old to safety, and then looked around for the other two. The 8-year-old was climbing up on the pier but there was no sign of the 6-year-old. He dove back into the water and searched for the missing boy. He found him, but after an extended amount of time all the efforts to revive him failed. Apparently when the canoe flipped it hit the boy in the head. After 30 years the memory still haunts him. Like "C's" experience, there is no way I can understand his grief.

When I asked a friend about her grief, this was her response: "First of all, let me state what grief was not for me. It was not a lack of faith. It was not a place, as it would come in waves. And, it certainly wasn't weakness. What I finally figured out was that I was mourning for myself, not him. My faith has taught me that he is in a better place, but I was left alone and had to recreate myself, so to speak. I had always considered myself a strong, capable woman. With him gone, I had to put my money where my mouth was and become just that. I guess I could say that grief has been a journey for me to find my 'self.' They say that there are stages of grief, and I was angry for the longest of time. But I let that anger spur me on to do what needed to be done even though I cried every time I saw his signature or handwriting. For the longest time I felt like I was in a fog. Sometimes I had moments of absolute clarity and other times not so much, making it difficult to make rational decisions."

Another friend related this experience. He was set up with his first date after the loss of his wife 18 months previous. The lady had also lost her spouse 4 years before. He said that as the evening progressed, he realized all he had done was talk about his wife. He apologized, saying, "I'm sorry, I guess I have not been a very interesting date. Please understand that I am very nervous and uncomfortable. You are my first date since she passed." She replied, "I understand, Tony, it has been a longer time for me. It takes time to heal. Until you're ready you should not let friends force you back into dating. You are just not ready."

He responded, "I am sure you are right. Here I have been talking about my wife all evening and should have asked you about your husband." She shared, "He had a very unexpected heart attack. It happened 4 years ago, and I have had time to adjust... But do we ever really adjust?" They parted the evening good friends and see each other occasionally as "good friends" for having shared the experience.

Following up on the question, "Do we ever really adjust?" I asked another friend whose husband had died three years ago. She considered the question and answered, "I used to lay awake at night tormented by questions that seemed to have no answer. No, I don't think I will ever adjust to his loss. I am a changed person, but I am still not over his death." It's kind of comforting to me, knowing that I am not the only one who has had a difficult time with grief.

Grief from a child's point of view is shared by a friend:

"As a youngster, I found grief to be confusing. I attended many viewings and funerals with my parents. The confusion that I experienced at this age was when I attended Sunday School. I was taught how wonderful Heaven was. The streets are paved with gold, I would live forever in the house of the Lord, and I'd eat from a table prepared for me by the Lord.

Why were people crying, was it tears of happiness? It certainly did not appear that way. Why wouldn't you want to go to heaven as soon as you could?"

"Then my beloved dog, Pepper, died. I could hardly catch my breath from the buildup of fluid in my throat and my eyes flooded with a pool of tears, and I couldn't eat or sleep. If I saw one of Pepper's dog toys it sent me into tears. Our house seemed cold and empty, no licks, no looking with those sorrowful eyes wanting what you were eating. No jumping up in your bed to protect you from the monsters under the bed. I learned when I was older that our pets give us unconditional love. This is why it hurt so much and for so long." She told me that some 75 years later, and she still has memories of Pepper!

Some would find it unsettling to hear a child talking about death but it's normal. They're obsessed with the "whys" of the world. They're trying to make sense of everything in the world around them… including death.

If you have a child experiencing grief, encourage them to talk about their emotions. Suggest other ways to express feelings, such as writing in a journal or drawing a picture. Without overwhelming the child, share your grief with them. Expressing your emotions can encourage them to share their emotions, and it will also help you with your grief.

It is said that children and older people (that would be me) ages 6 to 68 are more likely to see angels and demons. The reason why is they are closer to the spirit world.

I guess that this must be true because I have seen the demons in my dreams and also the angels. Joyce has been there, and it is certain she was always a guarding angel to her granddaughter and family and a saint for putting up with me.

Here is a list of what is considered to be the most common signs of Angels:

- Finding a White Feather
- Flashes of Light
- Rainbows
- Tingling Sensations, Goosebumps or Chills
- The Feeling of Being Touched
- Symbols and Images in Clouds
- Scents

I'm not sure if it was Angels, but I have experienced many of these since Joyce's death.

Then there are the pleasant memories like these:

I spoke with someone who I'll refer to as "J." His wife died 15 years ago from breast cancer. He shared this memory of their wedding. He said, "I dropped the ring and we both bent over to get it and banged our heads together hard. Hard enough that she almost blacked out. The priest stopped the ceremony so she could sit and regain her composure and readjust her veil. Along with family and friends we have laughed about it for years."

My friend from Florida who lost his wife of 47 years,

shared this memory: "After we retired to Florida, I wanted to go out one day and play golf. She did not play golf but wanted to drive the cart (mistake). I had walked up onto a green to putt when I heard my wife yell alligator! She panicked and ran the cart into a sand trap. She still had her foot on the accelerator, spinning the tires, burying the wheels in the sand. This is a moment I will never forget. It was not funny when we had to explain the incident to the pro shop, but our friends all got big chuckles and would bring it up to her occasionally."

I guess this is where I should share some of my memories. I have the balloon string and I am moving it to pleasant memories.

When talking with others who are grieving over a spouse, I like to hear stories that make people smile, so I always ask them to share the memory of their first date. Here, I would like to share the memory of my first date.

I had met Joyce a week before our first date on a Saturday, but I was involved in a serious relationship (I thought), and I was not looking for a girlfriend. About 3 days after that meeting, I received a "Dear Tom" (Dear John) letter. Obviously that serious relationship was not as serious as I thought!

On Thursday two of my friends called and said they had dates and were going to South Bend, Indiana, to see a movie and then go out for pizza. They wanted me to get a date and join them and suggested I call Joyce. After some arm twisting, I finally agreed to call her. At first she wasn't sure, but I told her that her friend Sandy was going and she accepted the date. After I hung up, I realized that I wasn't even sure what she looked like.

Saturday came and I offered to drive. I had a new Plymouth Valiant compact so it would be 4 in the back and two in front. I drove to my friend's house; both the guys were there so we decided to have a beer before we left to pick up the girls. We picked up their dates in Goshen and then drove to Elkhart to pick up Joyce. When we arrived at her house I was greeted at the door by her mother. She asked me to step in and as I did, I tripped and fell into her arms!! Yes, with beer on my breath! She managed to keep me from falling on the floor.

Her mother called Joyce and she came from her bedroom. Remember, I wasn't even sure what she looked like. But there she was in a cute little sleeveless dress, beautiful brown hair and gorgeous big brown eyes... wow! At that point I turned to her father and said, "We're going to a movie and out for pizza. We should be home by 11:00." I guess I thought this might help smooth over my grand entrance.

We went to the movie and then out for pizza. As we were leaving one of my friends asked if he could drive. I said sure, thinking now I will get to sit in the back seat close to her.

Since we had parked on a busy street, we entered the back from the passenger door side. I opened the door allowing Joyce to get in, and she moved to the far side next to the window and I followed. The other couple followed making it tight but nice!

We had traveled a few miles when suddenly Joyce yelled, "Unzip my dress!!" I was dumbfounded. The driver almost ran off the road and the other couple was gasping in disbelief. Joyce had turned her back to me and said, "Unzip my dress, there's a cigarette down my back."

It was August, a warm night, so we had all the windows open. Back then we all smoked and what happened was she tried to flip a cigarette out the window, but it came back in and went down the back of her dress.

I finally understood the situation and managed to unzip her

dress and get my hand down between her dress and slip. The cigarette was actually down between her slip and back. I managed to grasp it and was able to keep it away from her skin. By this time my buddy had stopped the car and we got out along the street. There I was standing on a city street with my hand down the back of a girl's dress.

I was burning my fingers until one of the girls managed to reach down between her slip and back and take the cigarette from me. We all got back in the car with everyone laughing at me because of my reaction when she said, "Unzip my dress."

You would think this was the end of the story, but there was more to come when we arrived at her house. I walked her to the door, and she insisted I come in so she could get some ointment for my fingers. I said it was not necessary, but she insisted.

She had to walk by her parents, who were watching TV, to the bathroom to get the ointment. She applied the ointment and then she walked me to the front door where we shared a kiss. She said, "Thanks for the nice evening." I replied, "Thanks for the exciting evening, and by the way, you better explain to your parents about the cigarette because your dress is still unzipped."

And that's the story from August 5th, 1961 (I found this date in her diary). We were married a year later on August 11th, and interestingly enough she died on August 5th, 2019. I would like to share with you what else she wrote in her diary August 5th, 1961, but I want to keep it just between the two of us.

Do you remember when you met your spouse, your first date, your honeymoon?

Update for Second Edition

During the last several months I have experienced a lot of "sharing." Toward the end of my presentations, I usually ask if there are any questions or comments. I get a few but after I finish, I always have a line of people wanting to "share." Many of the stories are the same but different, if that makes any sense. What I mean is we all have many of the same grief experiences but each in different ways. What I have learned is that it takes a great deal of courage to "share," and when we do share it eases the pain. As I said earlier, sharing helps us move forward with the love and memories but with less pain. The more I speak with people the more I understand how important is to "share."

"There is no grief like the grief that does not speak."
- Henry Wadsworth Longfellow

"A cheerful heart is good medicine,
but a crushed spirit dries up the bones."
- Proverbs 17:22

Chapter Seven

"Don't Stop Laughing"

"Never lose your sense of humor. Never stop laughing." My dad always told me this as I traveled through my life. He'd tell me this as I experienced the good times and the bad as a young man over the disappointments of growing up, and then later in life when I lost a job or experienced tough financial experiences. Now that I am going through the stress and grief of my wife's death, I remember his words. So, I must work to retain my sense of humor.

Laughing and having a good sense of humor may not cure us of all our grief problems but it can, however, boost our morale and it is even said to prolong our lives. We are all going to die, but we can choose to pursue humor and laughter as long as we live.

After Joyce's death I felt myself losing my sense of humor. Laughing had to almost be forced. Things that I had always thought to be funny no longer brought the smiles and chuckles. Like Sergeant Schultz on *Hogan's Heroes* with his catch phrase, "I see nothing," or the great humor from the characters on the TV show *M*A*S*H*, they just weren't that funny anymore.

Psychology tells us that every human being has a sense of humor, as it is a part of our inner system similar to hunger or feeling pain. However, a person can appear to lose their sense of humor if they go through a traumatic experience such as grief, which has broken them from the inside, so much so that they can't feel anything. This was me. Now what do I do?

I found that humor is a very subjective thing. It may be difficult to get back the same sense of humor you once had. It took time yet I began to regain my sense of humor, but things were different. Oh, Shultz and *M*A*S*H* are still funny and make me laugh. But what's funny, humorous and makes me laugh are now different. I can't really explain it, but it's just different.

It is hard to regain that sense of humor. What I found was when I was unable to handle and process the grief it was hard to make the kind of connections that humor requires. Humor results from those unguarded moments, and I was always on guard, protecting myself from the grief.

So, I did some research and in psychology there is the concept of the "Homunculus," a tiny watch keeper in your brain who has a safe. He watches every single thing that happens, that is said, and that is done, and when something happens that might upset you, he grabs it and puts it in the safe where you can't think about it. The problem is that the safe can only hold so much stuff and then every time he opens it to add another bad feeling, a memory escapes, forcing you to deal with it. In order to fix it you have to deal with the issues in the safe. You must take them out, feel the pain and deal with them. Get them in that "balloon" where you can control them.

As someone always said to me, "It is what it is, so deal with it." I learned the reason it's important to accept the things that happen is because it allows you to let your guard down. When you do that, you allow your mind to find the humor. Once you find humor and laughter again you will begin to find peace.

Grief causes tension, and people who are tense don't find much to laugh at. They are under too much pressure, afraid of doing or saying something wrong. In my early travel through grief, I was afraid to laugh, afraid how people might judge me. I was supposed to be mourning, sad and somber. Don't get caught here, take control and be yourself, not what others think you should be.

In order to laugh you have to approach things differently. No one wants to hang around with someone who is constantly being sad and somber. So, you need to move past that step and work on rebuilding your sense of humor.

So then, how does one move on? My recommendation is to seek those things that were always funny to you: TV shows, movies, books, etc. In order to regain your sense of humor you have to let down your guard and allow the unexpected to happen. Join your friends at social events, experience their sense of humor and let it help generate yours. By doing this you may not need Homunculus to protect you.

Maybe you can take those bad feelings and memories out of the safe and deal with them. Once they are gone, you can find humor again. Maybe it won't be the kind of humor you liked before, but instead a new kind of humor.

Update for Second Edition

As I have moved along my grief journey with her, with my balloon of memories, I have slowly regained, maybe I should say rebuilt, my sense of humor. In my speaking engagements and media interviews I have been able to relate the funny things along with the difficult times of the journey. I reflect back on the last thing she said to me, which was, "I love you, and I will see you in church." In my presentation I always ask the women if they can say a sentence to their husband without a command at the end. For example, "Hi, honey, how was work today? Would you please take out the trash." That is what Joyce did to me when she said, "I will see you in church." I go to church with a smile on my face thinking of her words. She and God probably get a good chuckle too. And the priest knows and will remind me of her words with a big grin. Yes, I can actually handle with a smile what was a very difficult time hearing her last words.

"Do not dwell in the past, do not dream of the future,
concentrate the mind on the present moment."
- Buddhist Quote

God will never abandon us during our time of grief.

Chapter Eight

"God Will Help"

God will help, just ask! God will not abandon you during your grief. He will always be there; all you need to do is go to him. He will provide you with the strength to face your grief.

"Blessed are those who mourn,
for they shall be comforted."
- Matthew 5:4

"The Lord is near to the brokenhearted
and saves those who are crushed in spirit."
- Psalm 34:18

God broke my heart when he took Joyce, and he certainly got into my heart. It took a while after her death to finally call on Him, but he was there for me. I figured out though that Joyce and God were in "cahoots" since her final words to me were: "I love you, and I will see you in church."

She was, as a convert, a much better Catholic than me, but with her death I have found a new understanding of my church and God. I guess like many people I sometimes allowed selfish motives to rule my life decisions. I am striving now to live the way she and God would want me to live. I am gaining more strength each day to do it "my way," which is Joyce's and God's way. I pray each day that He will give me the strength to cope with the grief and with my memories of her to build a new life. God is with you, even if you think you are alone. He's still watching over you.

With my grief and mourning has come a new appreciation and understanding of my Catholic faith. I have learned to pray with vigor and purpose. I have re-established my habit of daily prayer and meditation. I have found a new inner peace. I have discovered who I am, where I am, and what I need to be doing. Prayer has brought my life back into focus.

Prayer is not necessarily on your knees in church, although that works. It can just be sitting with your morning coffee planning your day in Jesus' footsteps, and then with that glass of wine before dinner and reflecting on your day. Did I do as Jesus would have done today? Was I compassionate and understanding of other people? Was I able to brighten someone's day in my conversation with them? Would Jesus say, "Yea, man, good job," or would he shake his finger at me in disapproval?

Prayer is not necessarily saying the "Our Father" or "Hail Mary," although these will also work. It might just be sitting on your deck or patio watching the sunset or sitting in front of your fireplace listening to peaceful music and talking to God. It is also a good time to talk with your loved one. They are probably standing right there next to God waiting to hear about your day. Tell them exactly as it was. If you experienced the pain of grief or the joy of pleasant memories, share it with them.

"The LORD is near to all who call on him,
to all who call on him in truth.
He fulfills the desire of those who fear him;
he hears their cry and saves them."
- Psalm 145:18-19

"Blessed be the God and Father of our Lord Jesus Christ,
the Father of mercies and God of all comfort."
- 2 Corinthians 1:3-4

If I continue to pray all my sorrow to God, he will replace it with hope, peace and joy. This I believe! When a loved one dies, the Church and funeral home supply you with information about grief and prayers. Following are some examples of those prayers:

"Consoler of the Grieving,
you know the pain of my loss.
Come with your compassionate love.
Embrace my sorrow and heartache.
Soothe my sore, distressed spirit."
- Author Unknown

"Beloved of My Soul
I bring you the pain of my loneliness
with its sharp edge of sadness.
I bring you the hollow place inside
that longs to be filled with love."
- Joyce Rupp*

---

* From *Prayers in Times of Suffering* © by Joyce Rupp
www.joycerupp.com, used with permission.

"Holy God, Your word says that You are a refuge for the oppressed, a stronghold in times of trouble. Lord, I call upon You to be my stronghold in my time of grief! I feel oppressed by the pain and the sorrow that I feel, but in You, I know that I can find peace for Your word tells me so. Awesome Father, please have Your divine way within my mind so that I can find comfort in this difficult time, Amen."
- Psalm 9:9

I decided these did not tell my story so here is my prayer, not as eloquent as Joyce Rupp's, but it is what I feel:

Give Me the Strength

Hey, God, you took my loved one
and I don't understand why.
She was a very good person
always ready to help those in need.
She was a very devout Catholic
much better than I.
Why didn't you take me
and leave her to continue the good.
Oh, wait, I think I understand.
You want me to take over
and be a good person like her.
Not sure I can do it, not without her strength.
Her saying, "It is what it is, deal with it."
Okay, but please help me.
God give me the strength.
Amen.
- Thomas L. Rose

Because grief and mourning can be so intensely personal, there are no prohibitions against Catholics using their own words to pray, which I have done with my prayer. Many people also turn to scripture in these times, reciting lines from the Bible that comfort them.

In his book *I Heard God Laugh**, Matthew Kelly challenges readers to try prayer as a central component of their life. He says, *"Choose carefully it is the biggest decision you will ever make."* I would also like to share this from his book: *"Until you discover God's playfulness you will not enter into the depths of spiritual life. Until you discover the playfulness of the child within, you will not discover the playfulness of God. Dance in the rain, play in the mud, lose track of time, and maybe you will find yourself lost in God, and found once and for all."*

I guess if we are "created in the image and likeness of God" he must laugh, cry, and feel pain. He must dance in the rain, play in the mud and lose track of time. How great it would be as Kelly says to *"discover the playfulness of God."* I am not there yet, but I am working on it.

I am sure God has a sense of humor. On the day of Joyce's funeral, we had asked a friend to do the readings. When it came time, he began reading the "prayers of the faithful" before the readings. The priest had to come over and correct him. He looked down at the casket and apologized to Joyce and said he was "a professional being directed by amateurs," which brought smiles and chuckles to the friends and family. I think I heard her laugh… or maybe that was God.

In Genesis it says, "God promised men that good and

---

* *I Heard God Laugh* by Matthew Kelly © 2020, Blue Sparrow, used with permission.

obedient wives would be found in all corners of the world, then he made the world round and laughed and laughed!"

God created us and in doing so created laughter. It is a great stress reliever so it will help with our grief. Many times, when that balloon touches a side of the box it brings back memories that make me laugh, and sometimes, laugh and cry at the same time.

One of the memories that makes me laugh (and cry) is of the "string and the turkey." For most of our 58 years we hosted holiday dinners: Easter, Thanksgiving, Christmas, etc. On Thanksgiving eve, we would begin our food preparations by working together. One of my jobs was to prep "the bird." I would clean it, stuff it with herbs and fruit, tuck the wings under and tie the legs.

In the process of tying the knot, I would ask for her assistance to hold her finger on the string so I could create a nice tight knot. She would oblige but would always comment, "Whose finger did you use when you tied your Eagle Scout knots?" I would say, "I think she was a cute little blond," and then we would laugh!

I probably give God and Joyce a good laugh every time I take a walk. I live close to the cemetery, and it is a very nice place to walk. When I stop at the family plots, I always take a quick look at our stone, which of course has her date of birth and death. My name and date of birth are already there, but I look to make sure the date of death is not there yet! God probably laughs and says, "Tom, I'm the only one who knows."

After the death of a spouse, you need friends to help with the grief... God is your best friend so let Him into your "new" life. Be His friend and share your thoughts with Him. Talk with

Him daily and He will guide you through your days of grief and help you build a new life based on the memories of the past.

God will never abandon us during our time of grief. He will help, all you need to do is ask! He wants to be your "Best Friend" so let Him in. He will be there whenever you need Him and He will give you the strength to face your grief "head-on." God is there so: Talk with Him. Laugh with Him. Dance in the rain with Him. Play in the mud with Him. Lose track of time with Him. Be his friend and find yourself in Him.

Update for Second Edition

Along my journey with this book and speaking engagements, I have met a lot of people and been involved in many interesting and enlightening discussions about grief and God. Many times the question has come up: *"Why does God allow bad things to happen?"* I believe now that he uses those "bad things," including grief, to make us better people. When I sat there with Joyce for three weeks in Hospice, I kept thinking why is God doing this, why is he making us both suffer? I now know that He was getting into my heart in order to make me a better Christian, more Christ-like.

I think it is important that we understand God doesn't cause everything that happens to us, sometimes he allows things to happen. Bad things sometimes occur because we have made bad decisions. Maybe decisions that were opposite of what was God's will for us. Can we blame God for these things? Sometimes He uses our bad decisions to teach us to be a better person. He can use disappointment and tragedy to teach us to find trust in Him for the hope and comfort we need. These experiences have taught me to have better understanding and compassion for those who are suffering.

Yes, God broke my heart, took my grief and turned it into a positive experience in my life. I now encourage people to face their grief with a positive attitude, to move forward with their loved one and God at their side.

"Say not in grief 'he is no more'
but live in thankfulness that he was."
- Hebrew Proverb

The Decision

Chapter Nine

"Journey of Grief"

I thought it might be helpful to any of you who are just beginning your grief journey if I shared my first 2 ½ year journey as best as I can remember. It might help with what to expect. Remember, though, everyone is different and may experience grief differently.

I think my grief began three weeks before she died on the Saturday evening when she said, "I want to go into Hospice, what do you think?" At that time she was already in the hospital. I told her it was not a decision I could make, but that it was her choice. We had just spent a whole week meeting with doctors discussing plan A, then plan B, and had just finished hearing plan C. These were all basically about how to solve the chest drainage problem. Nothing about the cancer that had spread from her chest to other parts of the body including the brain. I told her to think about it and we would talk about it the next day.

She had fought the cancer battle in 2004/2005 and won. Now she had fought for 2 ½ years when they had originally told her she had 6 to 9 months to live. But it appeared this battle was now over.

That Saturday night was the first time I felt that aching in my chest, like being stuck with a big knife. I did not sleep well and cried most of the night. Sunday we would surrender to the cancer.

Sunday morning I showered, dressed and tried to eat something but couldn't. I felt sick to my stomach. My stomach hurt and it felt like I had that knife in my chest again. I went to the hospital, and she was having her breakfast. She did not eat much, but I did get her to drink her tea. No mention of Hospice. I held her hand and she slept.

The family came in the afternoon/evening. After they had all left, she said I have made the decision. "I am tired, and I don't want any more chemo, radiation or surgery. I just want to rest." I did not say anything. I just squeezed her hand and kissed her on the forehead. We advised the nurse that we had made the decision for Hospice. She said someone would come in the morning to work out the details. With that I began my journey of grief.

That night I was confused and afraid. What was I going to do without her? Why was this happening to her? Why not me God?? I was trying to deal with the fact that the decision was made and the end would come soon. More tears, but I did sleep better knowing that the decision had been made. And as she would say, "It is what it is, so deal with it."

Monday the lady from Hospice came and explained how everything worked and said we had choices of going home or moving to the Hospice ward in the hospital. Joyce quickly said she wanted stay at the hospital, which surprised me. I had thought for sure she would want to come home. In fact, I had gotten up early and cleaned the house and put fresh linens on her bed (they are still there).

I believe after 2 ½ years I now know why she choose the hospital… she did that for me so I would not need to care for her medications, change bedding, help with bed pans, etc. And that makes me feel bad because I was a little upset that she didn't want to come home.

Later that day they moved her to the Hospice ward. I stayed with her until late evening. When I arrived home, I felt that terrible loneliness. This is the way it is going to be, and I will be alone the rest of my life. I still had the feeling of the knife in my chest, my stomach still hurt, and now I was facing life alone.

That night there was a terrible thunderstorm and for some reason I was afraid. I was having this terrible nightmare. There were two figures holding Joyce up to the rain-streaked window and she looked terrified. I would wake up and, of course, nothing was there.

On Tuesday the doctor explained what would happen over the next few days. I left the hospital late that evening arriving home to a quiet neighborhood and lonely dark house. I still had that feeling of the knife in my chest, my stomach still hurt, and that painful lonely feeling.

Wednesday, I talked with the doctor. He told me death could come at any time, but her vital signs were still strong. That day was when I began to stay with her all night and day. I took some sweat pants and shirts that I would change into at night.

I slept, as well as possible, in a lounge chair next to the bed so I could hold her hand. The family came in the late afternoons to relieve me so I could go home and check the mail and phone messages, eat, shower, and put on clean clothes.

The days went by slowly and everything seemed surreal, passing by in a blur. It was the same every day, the doctor would come in the morning and check on her. He and I would talk, and he'd say he was surprised about how well she was maintaining her vital signs. She had not had any nourishment since she entered Hospice. Nothing but water and the drugs to suppress her pain.

On the Thursday prior to her death family arrived and I went home to do my thing. When the family left that evening Joyce seemed very alert, and she told me our granddaughter Amanda had sung for her. Amanda has a beautiful voice, and she has appeared in musical productions from her high school and college days, as well as some other local theater productions. Joyce told me that it was wonderful and that the nurses and some patients had gathered outside her door to enjoy the concert.

As I said, she seemed very alert and wanted to talk. We talked about the family, and she told me there was a green bag in the closet that contained the items she wanted at the funeral home. No videos or photo displays.

That was a special night. She thanked me for what I had done to help her battle the cancer, and then said, "I love you, and I will see you in church." Those were her last words to me. Until her death on the following Monday she hardly ever opened her eyes.

That night a flood of emotions came over me. I could not think. It was like a panic attack, and I had no idea what to do. All I could do was hold her hand and sob.

On Monday, August 5th, my daughter-in-law had come to relieve me about 4:00 pm. I had gone home and just entered the house when she called and said the nurse said I should come back ASAP.

I don't remember driving back to the hospital. The nurse told me she was failing quickly and it would not be long. I held her hand and there was a little squeeze from her and then she was gone. The nurse confirmed her death and said I could stay with her in the room for as long as I wanted, but I told her

Joyce was no longer there and I wanted to go home.

On the way home I had a strange feeling, almost a feeling of relief. She was no longer in pain. The suffering for her was over. She was in heaven with God. I felt happy for her.

When I arrived home the family was all there with a lot of hugging and crying. They wanted to fix me something to eat, but I said I really wanted to just be alone and they understood. After more hugs and I love you's they departed, leaving me to continue my grief journey.

I poured a glass of wine, sat on my deck for 3-plus hours watching the sunset and remembering Joyce and the good times. I finally realized that I was exhausted, so I showered and went to bed. As I closed my eyes that balloon touched all six sides of the box and all the emotions came over me. The confusion, fear, frustration, love, grief, loneliness and sadness all came at one time! I guess I was lucky because I fell asleep quickly and slept for 12 hours. I don't remember dreaming.

The rest of the week I was busy with arrangements, contacting family, answering phone calls and having visits from friends. Everyone, of course, wanted to help in any way they could. I did not have time for grief, it would need to wait!

We set the funeral for Friday and the visitation for Thursday afternoon and evening. Thursday and Friday were long emotional days.

The visitation on Thursday is kind of a blur. I remember the four hours and 400 visitors went by quickly. Lots of hugs and people saying, "I'm sorry for your loss," etc., etc. At the end of the visitation the family and a few friends stayed for some prayers and the rosary. I believe I went out for dinner with the family, but don't really remember.

Friday, we went to the church about two hours before the

service and had more friends come to us with condolences. The closed casket, as it had been for the visitation (her request), sat at the back of the church. I had not seen her since her passing on Monday and was not sure I wanted to, but the rest of the family wanted a last view. I did take a quick look and was glad I did. The funeral home had done a nice job, and she looked like she was resting peacefully. So that image can be my final memory rather than the one from her death bed.

The service was beautiful. Amanda sang and our friend Father John gave a great homily about Joyce and her life. I mentioned earlier in the book about the humorous event with the readings. In the church when we say the "Our Father" we always hold hands. I was sitting at the end of the pew next to the casket and I felt her take my hand.

After the service we had no procession to the cemetery since she was being cremated and the burial would take place the following week. There was dinner at the church with more hugs and condolences. Afterwards we, the family and several friends, returned to my house and went on the deck for some "liquid refreshments." The last of the guests left about dusk and I remember hesitating to go into the house because I knew I was alone; she was not there.

I went to bed early and slept peacefully (probably because of the liquid refreshments). I had very pleasant dreams remembering our first date and our wedding. Awaking the next morning, I was refreshed and ready for my new life without her, or so I thought! But it didn't take long for the grief to begin to take effect. The aching in my chest returned, and it felt like someone was twisting that knife again. I was having trouble functioning. I had decisions that needed to be made. I was confused and not sure how to proceed. I finally, with the help of my family, managed to pull myself together and go to

Mass that evening. That night I did not sleep well. The pain was almost unbearable, the loneliness engulfed me, and I was afraid and feeling very sorry for myself all at the same time. My grief was building up to "full force."

I spent about 3 months in an "off and on" blur. Some days having no problems and then others having grief throw something at me. Sometimes heartache or loneliness, sometimes anger, fear or self-pity and sorrow. I found it very difficult at times to make decisions, simple decisions, or I was confused about how to proceed with my life. I also had times when I had pleasant memories, some that brought smiles and others that brought tears. Again, some that made me smile and laugh and others that made me cry.

After about three months is when I finally called on God to help me, to give me her strength to move forward. This is also when I discovered the "balloon in a box" and managed to grab that string and as best as I could started taking control of grief and my emotions.

When my friend suggested I write down my thoughts and feelings, I realized as I wrote that I was learning to control my grief, my good and bad days. Since then, I have concentrated on learning more about how to control that "balloon."

As I write this, it is the holiday season and Christmas is only a few days away. This will be my third Christmas without her. Each day I have developed better control of the string and balloon, so the holiday season is turning out to be a very good one with family, friends and my joyful memories of holidays past.

After almost 2 ½ years I still experience all the symptoms of grief which will be with me forever. Yes, I still cry, get angry, feel lonely, experience fear and confusion, feel the heartache and sorrow. But I now understand how to handle the grief and not let it rule my life. As long as I keep God as my "friend" and hang on to that string, I'm okay!

A doctor friend explained to me that a broken heart is forever, it will never heal. But it is like a broken leg that sometimes when the weather gets cold you feel the pain, but then you learn to dance with a limp.

Update for Second Edition

My journey continues and I have "learned to dance with a limp." My heart is still broken and just like Humpty Dumpty it can never be put back together, but I understand that I must continue my journey with a broken heart. I must do as she always told me, "It is what it is," so I must put on my "big boy pants and deal with it." Part of my dealing with it is learning to understand it.

*"With grief first comes the pain of loss and then
the challenge of moving forward with life."*
- Deacon Steve

Chapter Ten

"Creating A Grief Journal"

Dealing with grief is one of the biggest challenges one can face in life. At the suggestion of a friend, I found a grief journal was a way to work through the emotions. It helped me reflect on and deal with these feelings. It also led to the creation of this book. Maybe there is a book in you, and if not then I am very confident it will definitely help you with your grief. Here are the steps you can follow to begin your grief journal:

Understanding Why

When grief comes it's easy to bottle up the feelings. If you can't express yourself, you could end up not expressing anything at all. Feelings of loneliness and depression are common with grief. Holding on to these feelings can have a negative effect on you.

Over time it can take a toll on your body. It can lead to high blood pressure and create other physical problems in addition to the mental pressure.

A grief journal is a great way to release those feelings, process them, and let them go slowly over time. When you write about your grief, you will take a closer look at and begin to understand your feelings, and you will sleep better and learn to cope with the pain.

Creating Your Journal

Creating your journal doesn't have to be anything fancy. You can simply pick up a composition book at a local bookstore. You could also start a digital journal online or through a word processing application on your computer.

You may want to build a formal journal with individual sections for special notations, but I think the best way is to just write what you are feeling on a daily basis.

It doesn't need to be formal paragraphs or even sentences, just what you feel and think. Just make sure you're comfortable with the format.

Be Inspired

Don't try to be creative because it's hard to be creative when you're struggling with grief. Just write it down, whatever comes. Finding the inspiration and motivation to keep writing may be difficult in the beginning, but the more you write the more inspired you will become. Also reading what you have written previously will help.

Ideas & Prompts

Sometimes it is hard to get started and keep it going. Here are some ideas and prompts to help get you started with your writing, keep it going, and keep you focused:

1. How do you feel today? Describe that feeling.
2. Share a memory of your loved one.
3. Write down all the things your loved one used to say.

4. Write a message to your loved one.

5. Find a quote that speaks to you. See Chapter 12 "Quotes That Touch the Soul."

6. Find a song that speaks to you. As you saw earlier in the book I listed some that helped tell my story... find your song(s).

7. Write about what you miss.

8. Write about what you are going to do going forward.

A Schedule

Make a journaling schedule. When I did my journal, I made a notation in the morning which sometimes included a dream and then again in the evening before going to bed. If you don't set aside time, it's easy to forget it. You need to make it a priority. Create a schedule, daily, weekly, etc., that's realistic for your lifestyle. I promise the more you do it the easier it will become.

Read It

You will find that one of the best things about writing your grief journal is how valuable it is in coping with your grief, so read your writing. This may be difficult at first, but it can be a large part of the grieving process. When you read what you have written you will reflect on these feelings again, but with greater understanding. You might want to share passages with a family member, trusted friend, or you may prefer to just read it to yourself.

Coping with Grief by Writing

A grief journal is a particularly effective way to cope with the feelings of grief. The stages of grief take time, and writing a grief journal gives you a way of expressing and healing yourself. Writing about your feelings keeps you connected to your loved one and your memories.

My biggest fear after Joyce's death was that I would lose these memories. But writing about my feelings and thoughts has helped me keep those memories alive. My journal, which led to this book, will be part of me for the rest of my life and hopefully a cherished memento of the family for years to come.

*"Everything that has a beginning has an ending.
Make your peace with that and all will be well."*
- Buddhist Saying

*"Two are better than one because they have a good return for
their labor. If either of them falls down, one can help the other
up. But pity anyone who falls and has no one to help them up.
Also, if two lie down together, they will keep warm."*
- Ecclesiastes 4:9-11

Chapter Eleven

"It Takes A Village"
- by Brock T. Rose

It's been over three years since my mother died. There isn't a day that passes I don't think of her. I am 58 years old and will forever be my mother's boy. In this book you have read my father's story, his journey of grief. This chapter is a reflection of my experiences as I have traveled with my father introducing his presentation and his book to many people experiencing grief.

After writing the book, as he describes it, he caught lightning in a bottle. The speaking engagements, podcasts, and interviews started flowing into his life. One day the phone rang and it was my father. He said, "This is overwhelming, I need your help." I listened to him and realized it was going to take more than just him to keep the ball rolling. I agreed to help and thus began my journey with him through grief.

I quickly noticed that as we traveled and spoke to different groups, we encountered many, if not all of the people attending, were experiencing loneliness. I expected them to be lonely from the death of a loved one but thought they must have friends and clergy to help them in those times. Sadly, many of them did not and were truly alone on their journey. So, as we continued to do presentations and talk with people, I started telling them that their journey will take a village of people to help guide and encourage them. This is where this chapter begins.

In determining your village, use the 4F method:

1. Faith
2. Family
3. Friends
4. Future

Sounds simple, right? Well sometimes it is, sometimes it isn't. So let's explore the 4F method.

The first F is for **Faith**:

Faith, as defined in many dictionaries, is complete trust or confidence in someone or something. It is also defined as a strong belief in God and religious doctrines. Those are definitions that are open to a lot of questions.

Who do I trust? Who do I have confidence in? Do I have God in my life? What is my religious orientation? Answering these questions can help lead you to people and organizations that can help you in your journey. But what if you have no answers to those questions? I would suspect that many of you have never really thought about it.

Struggling with faith is normal, it's part of growing. I for one have struggled with my faith. I left my church and retreated to my safe place. I essentially kicked God and faith out of my life and moved on. One day I sat looking out the back window at my mother's gravesite (my home borders the cemetery), and I realized that even though I said I was moving on without my faith and God, I had gone nowhere. That was when I decided I was going to go back to church.

I had a nervous almost gut-wrenching feeling as I approached the entrance. It had been over 3 years, and I just hoped lightning didn't strike. I am Catholic as you may have assumed from reading my father's journey. So, as we Catholics do when we enter church, we dip our fingers in holy water and make the sign of the cross. It didn't burn me, and lightning didn't strike. Instead, I actually felt overwhelmed with peace and comfort. After the service I felt more at peace than I had in years. Since that first service I have allowed God back into my life and asked him to guide me along the way.

Let's look at the second F, **Family**:

I don't come from a big family; I have no brothers or sisters and my grandparents have all passed away. I was lucky to have my grandparents around as I was growing up, and I cherish the things they taught me about life. Every time I come to a hurdle in my journey, their wisdom has allowed me to jump forward and continue onward.

When my mother died, I turned to my loving wife Rose, daughter Amanda, and my son-in-law Chris. I can't thank them enough for their support and understanding. We all needed each other to get through the grief. We came together as a village and surrounded my dad with our support and love. Together we managed the grief and set out to discover our new 'normal.' There is no need to be alone on your journey. If you have family, seek their comfort. I know it may be hard as it sometimes can be with family, but true family will always be there for you when you need them most.

The third F is for **Friends**:

Sometimes this is the most difficult F. Funny, Facebook says I have 1,400 friends, but how many do I really have? Yes, I know, Facebook seems to be the place where we all air our laundry in hopes of getting smiling faces and prayer hands, and those are nice, but it's not what you need. Those messages and icons only last a short time, then they are gone. You need someone who is going to be there today, tomorrow and in the future.

As my dad said in this book, the griever needs three things: finding the words, saying the words, and knowing the words have been heard. As I thought about these three things, I found myself saying, "I have the words, I can say the words, but who will truly hear them?" I discovered that friends come in many forms and determining who I could trust and had confidence in was key. I had many friends who offered advice trying to fix my grief, but as we know it can't be fixed. Even more friends sent me messages of encouragement. Those were nice, but still not what I was looking for. In the end I found a handful of friends who would just listen, smile, and say, "I love you, and I am here for you." That's exactly what I needed.

Finally, we come to the last F, **Future**:

Now that I had put my village together with Faith, Family and Friends, it was time to look forward. I had my balloon tied to my finger, I put God at the wheel, and I loaded my family and friends in the car, but where to now? Wish I had the answer to that question. All I know is that I am not driving. I have my friends and family with me, and life is different than it was. I have become a better son, father, husband and friend. Maybe that's all you need. Let's face it, life isn't black and white. In order to enjoy it you need to explore it. What the future holds is up to my Driver, I am just along for the ride.

"Jesus wept."
- John 11:35

Chapter Twelve

"Quotes That Touch the Soul"

In doing research for this book, I found hundreds of quotes with references to grief and mourning. I have used several of these throughout the book, but I thought it might be good to share them again and a few more with you here.

This Chinese proverb is one of my favorites:

"You cannot prevent the birds of sorrow from flying over your head, but you can prevent them from building nests in your hair."

Here are some of the others which "touched my soul."

"There is a sacredness in tears. They are not the mark of weakness, but of power. They speak more eloquently than ten thousand tongues. They are the messengers of overwhelming grief, of deep contrition, and of unspeakable love."
- Washington Irving

"Tears are the silent language of grief."
- Voltaire

"Grief is the price we pay for love."
- Queen Elizabeth II

"The life of the dead is placed in the memory of the living."
- Marcus Tullius Cicero

"Tears water our growth."
- William Shakespeare

*"Why does it take a minute to say hello
and forever to say goodbye?"*
- Author Unknown

"What soap is for the body, tears are for the soul."
- Jewish Proverb

*"Perhaps they are not stars in the sky,
but rather openings where our loved ones shine down
to let us know they are happy."*
- Eskimo Legend

*"Although it's difficult today to see beyond the sorrow,
may looking back in memory help comfort you tomorrow."*
- Author Unknown

*"If tears could build a stairway, and memories a lane,
I'd walk right up to heaven and bring you home again."*
- Author Unknown

"Time heals old pain, while it creates new ones."
- Proverb

*"Love is like standing in wet cement,
the longer you stay the harder to leave and you can
never leave without leaving your marks behind."*
- Author Unknown

*"Every heart has its secret sorrows which the world knows not,
and oftentimes we call a man cold, when he is only sad."*
- Henry Wadsworth Longfellow

*"Honest listening is one of the best medicines
we can offer the dying and the bereaved."*
- Jeanie (Jenny) Cameron

"We get no choice. If we love, we grieve."
- Thomas Lynch*

---

* *The Undertaking* by Thomas Lynch © 2009, W. W. Norton & Company,
used with permission.

"Say not in grief 'he is no more'
but live in thankfulness that he was."
- Hebrew Proverb

"We need never be ashamed of our tears."
- Charles Dickens

"Some people come in your life as blessings.
Some come in your life as lessons."
- Mother Teresa

"The fact that something has happened to a million
other people diminishes neither grief nor joy."
- Author Unknown

"Lucky is the spouse who dies first
who never has to know what survivors endure."
- Sue Grafton*

"The comfort of having a friend may be taken away,

but not that of having had one."
- Seneca the Younger

"You left this world but not my heart."
- Author Unknown

---

* *"F" is for Fugitive* by Sue Grafton © 1989, Henry Holt and Co., used with permission.

"Her hug lasts long after she lets go."
- Author Unknown

"There is no grief like the grief that does not speak."
- Henry Wadsworth Longfellow

"Say not in grief 'he is no more'
but live in thankfulness that he was."
- Hebrew Proverb

"Everything that has a beginning has an ending.
Make your peace with that and all will be well."
- Buddhist Saying

I agree with most of these quotes, and they touched my soul deeply, as do my memories of Joyce. The following quote probably says it all. It wraps it up nicely, saying what it was, what it is and what we must do.

"Do not dwell in the past, do not dream of the future,
concentrate the mind on the present moment."
- Buddhist Quote

"It is what it is.
Put on your big boy pants and deal with it."

Epilogue

What I have done here in this book is share my grief experience and given you my views on the death of a spouse and grief. If you are reading this book because you are grieving, I hope that it has helped you with your pain. Please be aware I am not a doctor of psychology or a trained grief counselor. I am just me, plain old Tom Rose who lost Joyce, the love of his life. The reason I wrote this book is because most everything I read or was told is wrong. **Unless you have been there you do not truly understand.**

It has been 2 years and 4 months since Joyce died. I am entering the third holiday season without her, and it seems more difficult than the first two. We shared a lot during the season, decorating, shopping, wrapping gifts, cooking and family. The memories come as I decorate the house with her 110-piece Santa Claus collection and the 226 tree ornaments, many from vacations and travel.

There are times when I am concerned that I might forget any of the details about her or our 58 years together. I am sure that will not happen. I remember everything about her. Her big brown eyes, her sense of humor, her love of others and even her smell. The first thing I had to do was remove her clothes from the closet. Every time I went into the closet the "smell" would make me tear up.

I remember all her little sayings like, "It's all," when referring to something that was gone. And of course, "It is what it is… put on your big boy pants and deal with it."

I remember her strength as she led me through some very tough times. When my older sister told me she no longer wanted anything to do with me I cried. Joyce said nothing, she just held me tight. When my father and mother died, she did the same, no words just love.

I remember her anger when I screwed up, not many words but just the look!! Oh, and like all women, she remembered and would remind me if I was about to make the same mistake again.

Today I will get up and make myself some breakfast after which I will dress and make the bed, as we always did, and start my day. I will turn on the computer and check for any business emails, cookbook orders and proceed as required with the information. My son Brock will call to see how my day is going. Sometimes I will play golf or cards at the club. When I arrive home, I miss the inquiry, "Well, did you break the course record?" And if it was cards, "Did you win or lose?"

Later it will be time for me to face dinner alone. This was the time of day when we talked about everything. We would cook together or sometimes we took turns. When we did that the person not cooking would sit at the counter, usually with a glass of wine. In warm weather this would take place on our deck and outside kitchen, which meant I was probably cooking.

So many memories, the birth of our son, his marriage and the birth of our granddaughter, Amanda. All Amanda's plays and musical performances we attended together with great pride. Memories of holidays with the family, parties and dinners with friends. For example, the vacation to the Abaco Islands where my friend and I tried to convince our wives that in the Abaco Islands there were only ten donuts in a dozen since we each ate one coming back from the bakery, and then our trip to the Canary Islands where we walked down to the nude beach.

Yes, I remember it all and miss it so very, very much,
but I will never forget.

On August 5, 2019, a Rose faded from my garden,
but a new Rose blossomed in heaven.
It grows in God's Garden, nurtured by his care.
Memories of that Rose will forever linger in my heart.

Well, here I find myself at the end of updating my book with the experiences and lessons of the last several months. The speaking engagements where I have shared my grief journey with over a thousand people has certainly helped me with my grief journey. Meeting these people and sharing has been a real "kick." I am proud to say that I have made this my mission, my ministry, my quest, and I will continue on as long as I can and as long as people want to hear my story.

As you may understand, having my son join me in this quest has been a real "kick" as well. He does my speaker introduction and as he says, drives "Mr. Daisy." What could be better for a father in his old age?

If you can help us with our quest, please contact me by telephone at: (574) 596-6256.

Balloon in A Box

Acknowledgments

Having never written a book before, I could not have done it without a lot of help and encouragement from friends and family. So, I must recognize all those who helped me with the challenge.

Dr. T. J. Lewis, who had suggested that I keep a journal to help with my grief, and he was the one who challenged me to take on the project after reading my journal.
Thanks Doc, your friend always.
***Note: *Doc died on March 12th, 2022, two weeks before his 82nd birthday. "Rest in peace, my friend."*

Those Who Shared so openly their grief experiences. You helped me understand grief and the thoughts and ideas I needed to include in these pages.
Thanks for your invaluable contributions.

Fran, Barb, Patty, Bobbie, Gene and Marsha are "special friends" who provided their support. Their kind words of encouragement made me feel like a "real author."
Love and hugs to all.

Rebecca (Beckie) Tichenor for your expert editing. Your personal grief experience added a special depth of understanding to the project.
In your debt forever.

Father John, Father Bob and Father Tony for providing the spiritual direction to reach God and all His gifts.
Bless you all.

Paul Rabinovitch and the staff at CCB Publishing for making me look like a real author and my book a reality.

Rose, Amanda and Chris, the family, who have provided loving support and encouragement while I have been on my journey of grief. Without you I could not have written this book.
Love you guys a whole bunch.

Brock T. Rose, my son, who has provided all the formatting and graphic assistance. His love and respect have provided the foundation for this book. He has always been there for me and was not afraid to tell me I was going in the wrong direction. I am very proud to call him son!
Love you more than words can say.

Joyce and God who together have provided all the inspiration for the contents of the book. I have drawn on her strength and His love to understand grief and how to deal with it.
My love continues to grow for both.

About the Author

Thomas L. Rose, Tom Rose, was born in Peru, Indiana, November 21, 1940, to Norman and Donna (Hipskind) Rose. He has two younger sisters Jacquelyn (Rose) Roberts (deceased) and Jill (Rose) England.

The family moved from Peru to Goshen, Indiana, where he still resides. He attended St. John's Parochial School and Goshen High School graduating in 1958. He attended St. Joseph, Ball State and Goshen College.

He married Joyce Grissom in 1962. Their son, Brock, was born in 1964. Brock and his wife, Rose, have a daughter Amanda (Rose) McMahon who with her husband, Chris, live in the Goshen area.

Tom worked in advertising and marketing most of his life and actually still does today with his son, Rose and Rose Associates.

With his wife Joyce he co-authored two cookbooks, *Cooking Together Chinese Style* and *Cooking Together Quick and Easy*. They also hosted a cooking segment on the local Fox TV affiliate for 13 years. During that time, they toured the Midwest teaching cooking classes.

After his wife's death Tom, with help from his son, authored a third cookbook, *Cooking Together Revisited*, which is dedicated to Joyce with the proceeds going to the families of Breast Cancer Support Projects.

Tom, along with his family, produce a YouTube cooking

show, Cooking Together Generations, to help promote their Breast Cancer Support Projects. The website is:

www.cookingtogether.com

In addition to cooking, Tom enjoys playing golf and listening to all kinds of music. He takes great pleasure in cooking with the family and cooking for friends.

Asked about the future he answered, "At 82 years old you are not really sure how much time you have left, but I hope the family and I can keep working on Cooking Together Generations and expand our Breast Cancer Support Projects. I also would like to do some more cookbooks and books like this, but that is all in God's hands."

Note from the Author

I once heard an older gentleman say,
*"No one really cares about my opinions,
but I am old so I continue to share them."*

The world didn't and you didn't ask for my opinion on "grief," but I gave it here in this book anyway. It was great therapy allowing me to share my feelings, memories, and also my opinions. The other day someone commented after reading the draft copy of the book, that it would probably bring me "fame and fortune!"

I am not looking for "fame" from this book, but maybe a little "fortune" that could help fund the family's Breast Cancer Support Projects. No, I am just looking for balance in my life. As I said in the book, the ability to move forward with my life with her, not without her, is my goal. Having time to do the things I enjoy and sometimes just doing nothing at all.

To me this book would be a success if I helped just one person coping with their grief. Thank you for taking the time to read this book, and I would love for you to share your thoughts and opinions. Check my website:

www.ThomasLRose.com

or email me at:

roseandrose@comcast.net

Sources

www.quotemaster.com

www.bbc.co.uk/bitesize

www.mygriefassist.com

www.elliesway.org.

www.imotions.com/blog feelings-emotions

www.counseling.online.wfu.edu

www.psychologytoday.com

Unexpected by Christine Caine, Zondervan, 2018

Prayers in Times of Suffering, Joyce Rupp

Joyce Rupp is well known for her work as a writer, international retreat leader and conference speaker. She is the author of numerous bestselling books distributed by The Servants of Mary, www.osms.org www.joycerupp.com

I Heard God Laugh by Matthew Kelly, Blue Sparrow 2020

Life is Messy by Matthew Kelly, Blue Sparrow 2021

Matthew Kelly is an internationally acclaimed speaker, author and business consultant. His books have been published in more than 25 languages, have appeared on *The New York*

Times, *Wall Street Journal*, and *USA Today* bestseller lists, and have sold more than 50 million copies.

Please check out his books and videos at:

www.matthewkelly.com

Joyce E. Rose

Joyce E. Rose, 78, Goshen, died 5:35 p.m. Monday, August 5, 2019, at Goshen Hospital. She was born July 23, 1941, in Elkhart, to Clell and Viola (Roberts) Grissom.

On Aug. 11, 1962, she married Thomas L. Rose. Surviving is her husband, Thomas; son, Brock (Rose) Rose; and granddaughter, Amanda Rose, all of Goshen.

Preceding her in death are her parents and an infant brother.

Joyce was a 1959 graduate of Elkhart High School and of the Elkhart School of Radiology. She worked as an x-ray technician in Goshen and Elkhart and retired in 1975.

Joyce, along with her husband, Tom, authored two cookbooks, Cooking Together with Tom & Joyce. They hosted a cooking feature on FOX 28 morning show for 13 years and taught cooking classes throughout the Midwest.

Joyce was a member of St. Mary of the Annunciation Catholic Church, Bristol, Daughters of the Revolution (DAR) and Delta Tau Delta Sorority.

Journal Notes

Journal Notes

Printed in the USA
CPSIA information can be obtained
at www.ICGtesting.com
BVHW041025310723
667996BV00001B/10